9 781300 584162

When Mosquitoes Come Marching In

A Play in Spectacles by M'Bha Kamara

NoPassport Press

When Mosquitoes Come Marching In by M'Bha Kamara

Volume Copyright 2021.

Contact the author at medchev@gmail.com for performance rights and other inquiries.

Cover photo: Yaroslav Maltsev. Vo6GqLo62HA_unsplash

NoPassport Press
PO Box 1786
South Gate, CA 90280 USA
www.nopassport.org

First Edition

ISBN: 978-1-300-58416-2

DEDICATION

To the children of Sierra Leone
who, because of the greed of
adult mosquitoes, have been
robbed of their dreams of a future;

to the children of Africa and the world,
who daily suffer a similar fate;

and to all those who work night and day
to make the world mosquito-free
for our children, our future,
I dedicate this humble effort.

ACKNOWLEDGEMENTS

This play carries my name as its author; yet, it would never have been without the kindness and support of so many. I would like to thank my mothers, Adama and Kadiatu, and my fathers, Sheka Bangura and Foday Momoh, for making everything possible. I give special thanks to my wife and friend, Tida Dramé, for her unconditional love and presence. Thank you to my kids, Luba, Adama, and Musa for putting up with my endless stories about growing up in Sierra Leone.

I am thankful to my older brother, Kelfala, for being there from the start and keeping me rooted in family; my brothers, Umaru Bah and Mohamed Kanu, for their unwavering intellectual and moral succor throughout; James Arthur-Yeboah for believing in me in those early days in Kono; Eric Sellin for his friendship and indefatigable mentorship; and to Pede Hollist for his honest and critical reading of an early draft of this play.

I am grateful to many colleagues at Washington and Lee University, including Domnica Radulescu for her enthusiastic endorsement of the play and for pointing me to Caridad Svich and NoPassport Press, Mark Drumbl for edifying conversations and collaborations on issues of human rights and child soldiers, Roger Crockett for encouraging me many years ago to publish this play, Erich Uffelman for his time and intelligence, and Shirley Richardson for always saying my stories are worth telling.

Setting:
West Africa, mostly the land called Salone.

Time:
A time not too long ago.

Dramatis Personae:
(In order of appearance)
Mr. Joe, teacher at the Sefadu Secondary School (SSS)
Class, Form 3 at the SSS
James, Munda, Sallay, Marie, students at the SSS
Samson Buake (also known as *Anophelius*)
Mr. Morseray, school bursar at the SSS
Samson's mother
Samson's father
Paul, also known as *Pot*, Samson's friend and classmate
Tamba (also known as *T-Boy*), Samson's classmate
Jamal, a prominent diamond dealer in Salone
Jimmy, Jamal's henchman
Alusine, a diamond miner
Hawa, a young woman, Samson's girlfriend
Honorable Minister, a member of the Salone parliament
Lamin, Honorable Minister's chauffeur
World Broadcasting Corporation (WBC)
Boima, Samson's friend in Monrovia
Say Bana, rebel leader
1st Heart
2nd Heart
Angel, a rebel fighter, assistant to Anophelius
Journalist, a WBC reporter

Guard, Honorable Minister's home security guard
Fighters, rebel fighters
Captain Kut'an, also known as *Albalau,* a rebel fighter
Killgore, a rebel fighter
Man, a captive of the rebels
Dogbowusu, a girl rebel fighter
Girl, a captive of the rebels

"Mosquitoes have a peculiar motto inscribed in characters of fire on a banner whose color blends with the darkest of tropical nights. Their war cry?

    'Blood for blood

    Rank for rank!'

None across the African continent can have peace of mind no sooner this war cry resounds in the distance at sunset. At first, it buzzes on the edge of the forest, then creeps toward human agglomerations with the slowness but implacable sureness of a volcanic lava."

Mamadou Gologo, *Le Rescapé de l'Ethylos* (my translation from the original French)

ACT I: "Once Upon a Time"

Spectacle 1

It is 8am, the start of 1ˢᵗ period in Form 3 at the Sefadu Secondary School. Mr. Joe, a geography teacher known to the students as Poyo Joe because of his addiction to mampama, *is pacing in front of the class while rhythmically tapping a 12" metal-edged ruler against his left palm.*

Mr. JOE: Good morning, class.

CLASS (*Almost inaudibly*): Good morning, Poyo Joe.

Mr. JOE: What was that?

CLASS (*Aloud*): Good morning, Mr. Joe.

Mr. JOE: Good! Do you know what we have this morning, class?

CLASS: No, Mr. Joe.

Mr. JOE: We have hot mental. Yes, you heard me right; hot mental. You know what hot mental is, don't you?

CLASS (*Rather despondently*): Yeessa.

Mr. JOE: I will repeat my rules of hot mental for those who have leaky brains. First, the surprise factor: I call you at random. Second, I ask, you answer. Third, you have two seconds between my question and the start of your answer. Fourth, once you have started your answer, you have three seconds to complete it. Fifth and final rule: you get your answer right, I move to the next person or I ask you another question; you get your answer wrong, your fingers will bear the wrath of the metal side of my ruler. Are the rules clear?

CLASS (*Examining the tip of their fingers*): Yes, sir.

Mr. JOE: I repeat: Are the rules clear?

CLASS: Yes, sir.

Mr. JOE: Good. Let the games begin. James, "How are volcanoes formed?"

JAMES: "Volcanoes are formed from magma ejected deep from the core of the earth due to intense heat and…."

Mr. JOE: Correct, James. You, Munda, "What is shifting cultivation?"

MUNDA: Shifting cultivation. It is the removal of land from one place to another place, sir.

Mr. JOE (*Whacks him on his bunched fingers*): Wrong. Sallay, "What is the capital of Honduras?"

SALLAY: It is…. I know this one. Yes! It is Egusi guava.

Mr. JOE: Incorrect! Your fingers.

Mr. JOE: Marie, the capital of Honduras.

MARIE: Tegucigalpa, sir.

Mr. JOE: Well done, Marie. Samson, where is Senegal located? In the Sahara or in the Sahel?

SAMSON: In the Sahel.

Mr. JOE: When did the Hut Tax War take place?

SAMSON: The Hut Tax War took place in 1898. And Bai Bureh...

Mr. JOE: "The imaginary axis at which the earth rotates remains inclined at an angle of _____ to the plane of earth's orbit."

SAMSON: But Mr. Joe, is that a geography question?

Mr. JOE (*Strikes him on the head with the ruler*): Shut up and answer the question, Samson. Hot mental rule # 2. I am the teacher, so I am the one who asks the questions here. And you, the student, the underling, are the one who answers my questions. You know what your problem is, Samson? You think you are smart. Maybe you are. But do you know what you really are, especially in my class? A cipher. That's what you are, a cipher. And that's what you will be your whole life if you don't change your attitude. So answer my question or…

The classroom door opens abruptly. In comes Mr. Morseray, the school bursar, carrying a sheet of foolscap paper between his thumbs and forefingers.

Mr. MORSERAY: If you permit me a brief interruption, Mr. Joe, I am here to conduct important school business.

Mr. JOE: By all means, Mr. Morseray.

Mr. MORSERAY (*He turns to the class*): Come forward when you hear your name. Finda Moigua, Momoduba Kamara, James Sesay, and Samson Buake.

The four students come forward.

Mr. MORSERAY: Do you know why I have called you out in front of the class?

SAMSON et al: No, sir.

Mr. MORSERAY: I called you out because you haven't paid your school fees. This is week five of the term, and you still haven't paid your fees. How many times do I have to tell you this school is not an SOS

Children's Village? If you need free education this is not the place for you. You should have asked to be born in the USSR. Now, I want you to go home, and do not even think of coming back until you have your fees. Out you go!

The students pick up their bags and books, and then exit the classroom.

Mr. MORSERAY (*Moving toward the door*): Thank you, Mr. Joe.

Mr. JOE: You are welcome, Mr. Morseray. (*He turns to the class*) Where were we? Oh, yes, Fallah...

<u>Spectacle 2</u>
A small cement brick building with corrugated zinc roof. Samson's mother is cooking on a three-stone fireplace in front of the house.

SAMSON'S MOTHER: Isn't it too early to be back home from school, son?

SAMSON: It is, mother. But I have been expelled.

SAMSON'S MOTHER: Expelled? Why?

SAMSON: Because I haven't paid my fees.

SAMSON'S MOTHER: How come? I thought your father gave you the money last week.

SAMSON: He didn't. Maybe he forgot.

SAMSON'S MOTHER: Well, he is in the parlor finishing his breakfast. You'd better go ask him now before he leaves. These days he leaves the house at the earliest opportunity.

Samson goes into the house to talk to his father.

SAMSON'S FATHER: What is it, Samson, don't you have school today?

SAMSON: I do.

SAMSON'S FATHER: So why are you still at home?

SAMSON: I just came back from school. I need my school fees. I was told not to return to school until I have my fees.

SAMSON'S FATHER: School fees? Why didn't you remind me?

SAMSON: I reminded you two weeks ago, and you told me to wait.

SAMSON'S FATHER: Well, it doesn't matter. Unfortunately, you are going to have to wait a little bit more. I do not have money right now. I will give you the money for your fees as soon as I have it.

He finishes his breakfast and leaves. Samson goes back outside to his mother.

SAMSON'S MOTHER: What did your father say?

SAMSON: He said I should wait.

SAMSON'S MOTHER (*To herself*): Once he has finished spending money marrying his new wife, he may have some change left over to pay your fees.

SAMSON: What did you say, mom?

SAMSON'S MOTHER: Oh, it is nothing. I was just reminding myself of something I have to do.

<u>Spectacle 3</u>
Downtown Kwedu. Samson and two other boys emerge from the movie auditorium at Morta Theatre, talking animatedly about the film they have just seen.

SAMSON: Man, was that a good movie or what!

TAMBA: Wow!

PAUL: Rambo is the best hero I have ever seen. Action from start to finish.

SAMSON: Yeah. Green Beret, Vietnam Veteran, war hero, Congressional medal... I want to be like Rambo.

14

Expert in guerilla warfare. Decorated with medals. Did you see how he operated that M-60 gun at the end? TdTdTdTdTdTdTdTd!!

TAMBA: Wow!

PAUL: "I could have killed 'em all, I could kill you. In town you're the law, out here it's me. Don't push it. Don't push it or I'll give you a war you won't believe. Let it go. Let it go." After Rambo said that, you know King shit cop Sheriff Teasle is in trouble. Big trouble.

TAMBA: Wow!

PAUL: Is that all you have to say, 'wow'?

TAMBA: Wow!

SAMSON: You know T-Boy. That's all you're going to get out of him.

PAUL: Never mind. (*Turns to Samson*) Hey, man. When you coming back to school? We miss you.

SAMSON: Why are you talking like that?

PAUL: Like how?

SAMSON: 'Hey, man. When you coming back to school?' Talking like you are American.

PAUL: Just imitating those guys in the film, dammit!

The three boys laugh heartily.

TAMBA: Wow!

They are now completely outside of the building and close to the street.

PAUL (*Pointing to a Mercedes parked on the street*): Look at that!

SAMSON: What?

PAUL: That car.

SAMSON: Oh, that! Yeah. Mercedes Benz 190. That's the latest model.

PAUL: If you die in a car like that, you will go straight to heaven. No joke.

TAMBA (*He moves to touch the car*): Wow!

JAMAL: Don't put your filthy hand on my car!

Startled, the three boys turn around in unison, coming face to face with a man they all recognize as a well-known businessman.

SAMSON: We are not doing anything to your car, Mr. Jamal. We are only admiring it. It is a beautiful car.

JAMAL: Don't say my name. Do I know you?

SAMSON: No, but it doesn't matter.

JAMAL: So fuck off then.

TAMBA: Guys, let's get out of here.

SAMSON: But we haven't done anything wrong.

JAMAL: Better listen to your friend, young man; he is giving you good advice.

PAUL: Come on, Samson. T-Boy is right. Let's go.

SAMSON: You can leave if you want. I don't have to.

Tamba and Paul move a few feet away from the car. Samson stands his ground.

JAMAL: Jimmy, get this rubbish out of my sight.

A stocky fellow materializes, grabs Samson by the collar, and shoves him away from the car.

JIMMY: You better get out of here.

Paul and Tamba pick Samson up and drag him away as he hurls invectives at Jimmy and Jamal.

<u>Spectacle 4</u>
Several months later. Samson is sitting at the edge of a pit, next to an older man. They are both shirtless, with their sweat-draped torsos glistening in the mid-day sun. Samson is nibbling on a piece of kebe *while the man smokes a Gauloise.*

ALUSINE: How is that kebe?

SAMSON: Nothing close to Mr. Komba's kebe. Its food, you know. Just like medicine, you don't always have to like food; you just eat it to stay alive.

ALUSINE (*Taps Samson jovially on the back*): That's the spirit, young man.

SAMSON: You know, brer Alusine, we have been working for too long with nothing to show for it. First at Kania, then at Kweyor, and now here at Yomandu. When are we going to have our first decent piece of diamond so we can at least buy a pair of nice shoes?

ALUSINE: Good question, Samson. But I believe that is a question for God. Do you know how many times I have asked Him that question?

SAMSON: No! How many times?

ALUSINE: Well, I left my hometown of Kiampudee in the north when I was 14 or 15 years of age. I am about 30 now. I have lived in the same room with my wife and two children for the past five years. I remember when I first came here. It feels like a lifetime ago! I was all hope and energy. I dreamt of returning home within a few short years, triumphant. In my village, there was a beautiful compound. Fenced, with a large metal gate. It was the most beautiful place I had ever seen. It had the only concrete building in my village. My dream was to come to Sefadu, find a big diamond quickly, and return to build a compound like it, if not more beautiful, for my parents. Don't get me wrong. I still have plenty of hope, even if my energy reserve has gotten a bit low of late. As for you, you only just started. You are young and strong. All you need is one day and one diamond. Who knows, school may no longer matter.

SAMSON: But I really want to be in school. That is the only reason I am here: Get a diamond that will allow me to return to school next year, since school is out of the question for the rest of this year. So I need to work extra hard.

ALUSINE: Well, what are you waiting for? Let's get back to work then.

WORLD BROADCASTING CORPORATION: "Brigadier General Sahid Binkolo has been picked by President Stephane Probert to be his successor as head of state of Salone. According to a leader of the long-disbanded Union of Sierra Leone Students, Probert has chosen the politically inexperienced military man as his successor because he prefers a successor he can control."

ACT II: "A Time Not Too Long Ago"

<u>Spectacle 1</u>

A few years since the last spectacle. Kwedu Town. Mid-August. Twilight. It is raining. A young woman, between 17 and 20 years old, is walking up a potholed street. A small multicolored umbrella open over her head. Some of her braids are fairly undone at the ends. Her Holland waxed lappa *is firmly held in place between her thighs with her left hand. She walks with practiced steps. She stops abruptly. Transfixed. In front of her, an enormous pothole full of water. Behind her, from the top of the narrow street, a car is bearing down on her. She regains her composure just in time to jump to the side of the road. Large flakes of muddy water explode on her entire body as the car speeds by. A few meters down the street the vehicle screeches to a tumultuous halt. Then Hawa notices that the sleek grayish Pajero, with heavily tinted windows, is reversing recklessly toward her. A back window rolls down about six inches. A voice comes through it.*

HONORABLE MINISTER: Can I give you a lift?

HAWA: No, thanks. I am fine.

The car continues to move to keep pace with Hawa who has not stopped walking.

HONORABLE MINISTER: Something tells me you don't live around here. Look at you. You have not even complained about your clothes. Give me at least

21

the chance to help you. I am sure you don't want to walk home in that condition.

HAWA: It is not a problem. I am used to it.

HONORABLE MINISTER: Used to what?

HAWA: To walking around in wet and muddied clothes during the rainy season. Cars drive by and splash us all the time.

The car stops and the window rolls all the way down.

HONORABLE MINISTER (*Pointing to the clouds*): You see those? They are getting darker. You know what that means, don't you? The rain will only get heavier. Open the back door for her, Lamin.

HAWA: (*Not looking at the minister*): Since I am already soaked, it doesn't make a difference now; I will just walk home. Besides, I don't know you.

HONORABLE MINISTER: I am sure you know me. Who does not know me? I am surprised you cannot tell who I am from my voice. You may not have recognized me because I am in a new car. If I were in the Mercedes Benz 124 that everyone here knows, you certainly would have recognized me.

HAWA (*She looks up at the clouds. Folds her umbrella, shaking the water off. She mutters to herself as she enters the car*): Well, I guess there is nothing to lose.

HONORABLE MINISTER: So you know who I am now?

HAWA: Yes.

Hawa sits somewhat awkwardly beside the minister. Her nose twitches at the overwhelming smell of new leather and the pungent odor of musk.

HONORABLE MINISTER: What is your name?

HAWA: My name is Hawa.

HONORABLE MINISTER: Where do you live?

HAWA: Nyandebo Street.

HONORABLE MINISTER: I know Nyandebo Street; it is nowhere near here. I used to have a girlfriend there. Useless girl! Anyway, on foot, by the time you get there, it will be dark and you will be miserably wet, cold, and dirty. Do you live alone?

HAWA: No! I live with my man.

HONORABLE MINISTER: What does that mean, "my man"? Are you married to him?

HAWA: No.

HONORABLE MINISTER: Then he is not your man. He is your boyfriend. What does he do?

HAWA: Nothing. Nothing at the moment.

HONORABLE MINISTER: And You? What do you do?

HAWA: I am a petty trader.

HONORABLE MINISTER: So you are the one who takes care of him?

HAWA: For now.

HONORABLE MINISTER: That is the problem with this country. The young men refuse to finish school, and they don't want to work. All they do is rob hardworking citizens, run after our women and girls and suck them like leeches. I suspected one of having an interest in my wife. Do you know what I did? I just called my friend, the Director of Central Prison. By the time he comes back out of that rat hole he will have learnt his lesson not to touch or even look at anything that does not belong to him. Has your man, I mean your boyfriend, tried to find work?

HAWA: He has tried. But there is no work. The only work available, especially in this area, is in the diamond mines. And he is tired of digging the earth for nothing. He is thinking about going into hairdressing or dancing. He is a good dancer.

HONORABLE MINISTER: Hairdressing or dancing? That's no work for a man. There is work everywhere in this country. Look at me. I have work. How do you think I got what I have today? I was not born rich. I wasn't born Honorable Minister. My parents were poor, and so were their parents. You don't get to where I am today by being lazy. In addition to the Mercedes Benz and this Pajero, I have another private vehicle, and two houses. As you probably know, I am building my new house not far from Nyandebo Street. In fact, that is the reason I am here. Otherwise, I don't like coming to this place.

He stops, looks at the woman as if to invite a question.

HAWA *(Disinterested)*: Why?

HONORABLE MINISTER: Why what?

HAWA: Why don't you like coming here?

HONORABLE MINISTER: This is a backward place. The roads are bad. In the dry season, my cars are covered in dust, and in the rainy season like now, it is the *potopoto*. And that aggravates me. I have visited many cities all over the world. No town in this country, not even our *alaki* capital, Freetong, can compare to any of those cities. I feel ashamed whenever I come back home from my trips abroad. Moreover, the people here are lazy and expect me to do everything for them. They have to remember that I am only their representative in parliament; I am not the government. (*Brief pause*) By the way, why are you still with this boyfriend of yours?

HAWA: I love him, and he loves me too.

HONORABLE MINISTER: Love, love, love! What does love have to do with anything? Everyone talks about love nowadays, just like White people. Even people who have never darkened the walls of a school talk about love. What every beautiful woman like you deserves is not a man who sucks his living out of her like the mosquito sucks blood out of poor people, while buzzing all the time "I love you, I love you." What I want to tell you is that I love you. The moment I saw you walking up the street, I said to myself "There goes a pretty girl. The kind a man would kill for." So, what do you say? Will you let me improve your life?

HAWA: I am fine with my life.

HONORABLE MINISTER: From the way you said it, I know you are not. Who in this world does not want a better life? If your man really loves you, he will do anything to give you everything you desire. You go to bed every night and dream of a better life. Don't you?

Hawa doesn't say anything.

HONORABLE MINISTER: Well, *tidae na yu dae*! After this very minute, if you wish, you will suffer no more. I will give you everything you want. All you need to do is say yes to me.

HAWA: I do want a better life. However, I am with someone already. Besides, you are married.

HONORABLE MINISTER: Of course I am. So what? Is marriage a chain around my neck and feet? Who says that because I am married I can't enjoy myself? *Bo duya*! Don't worry about my wife. As long as I feed, clothe, and house her, she should be thankful. If I am with you and she doesn't like it, she can pack up her things and leave. So what do you say?

HAWA: I don't have anything to say. I will…

HONORABLE MINISTER (*Cutting her off*): I am a very busy man, young woman. I am an honorable Member of Parliament and Minister, in case you have forgotten. I leave for Freetong tomorrow afternoon for an important meeting, so you have to give me an answer by tomorrow morning. I am sure you don't wish to kick your good luck away with your left foot.

The vehicle approaches the end of a street, about twenty or so meters from a house with No 43 Nyandebo Street charcoaled onto it.

HAWA: You can drop me off here. Thank you for the lift.

HONORABLE MINISTER (*Throws a few bank notes onto Hawa's lap as she opens the car door*): I will send my driver to pick you up in the morning.

HAWA: But I didn't…

The car speeds away. The rain has completely ceased by now. In the eastern horizon, nonetheless, new dark clouds have already begun to coalesce. It is almost night.

Spectacle 2

A tall, lanky man, easily recognized as Samson is standing by an open window overlooking the wet, almost deserted street a few feet away. The room behind him is rather spare. On the wall facing the window, held in place with sellotape, is a large outdated made-in-Nigeria calendar featuring Michael Jackson, Yvonne Chaka Chaka, MC Hammer, Sade, and other black artists. To the left of the calendar hangs a one-by-two rectangular mirror, and to the right, an adjustable wooden wall hanger. Against an adjacent wall is a full size bed topped with an oversized mattress stuffed with dry elephant grass, insufficiently redeemed by a worn gara bedspread. In one corner, a metal chair and a small desk atop which are a short wave Trident radio cassette player, a few cassette tapes, some bottles of body lotion and hair cream, lipsticks, eye browns, etc. To the right of the table, a shuku blai *with an assortment of pots, pans and spoons.*

SAMSON *(Still surveying the street)*: Where have you been?

HAWA *(Stowing her umbrella away behind the door)*: I have been to see my mother. You know she has been complaining a lot lately … "my head," "my stomach," "my knees," etc. I am worried about….

SAMSON *(Cuts her off as he turns to face her)*: I have not asked you about all that. Are you sure you were at your mother's?

HAWA: Why should I lie? If you don't believe me you can ask Anna-Mariya; I went there with her.

SAMSON: I am not going to ask any Anna-Mariya. "If you don't believe me ask Anna-Mariya!" What truth will come out of the mouth of a *raray gal* like her!

HAWA: She is not a prostitute. Don't call her a prostitute. She is my friend. Why do you like to bad-mouth other people?

SAMSON: Who doesn't know Anna-Mariya? Hasn't she slept with all the men in this area?

HAWA: All the men including you. Otherwise, how would you know?

SAMSON: Why would I sleep with a woman like her? Even though, as the saying goes, *doti wata sef kin ot faya*, she is not my type. I have always wondered what you do in her company. Alas, as Santigie Bombastic used to say, "Birds of identical plumage congregate in high proximity."

HAWA: Are you calling me a prostitute, too? Don't call me a prostitute.

SAMSON: Yes, I am calling you a prostitute. What is a woman who mingles with prostitutes? You sleep with hens you wake up with hen lice. Do you think I can't see what is going on?

HAWA: Nothing is going on, except in your head. If you don't believe I was at my mother's you can go there right now and ask her.

SAMSON: Stop telling me to go ask people about your whereabouts when you know you are lying to me. Your mother, like Anna-Mariya, will always back you up; she knows what you are doing.

HAWA: I am not doing anything. And keep my mother out of it. You have no respect for anyone, not even your own mother. If you had respect for your mother, you wouldn't say disrespectful things about my mother.

SAMSON *(He moves close to the woman and pokes her forehead with his forefinger as he speaks)*: Yes, I will say them, and no one will stop me. In fact, I will go further and say she is the one selling you to people with money and power.

HAWA: Maybe that is what your mother is doing; auctioning off your sisters to the highest payers.

SAMSON *(He slaps her on her right cheek, and kicks her in her belly)*: What makes you think you can talk about my mother like that? Enh? You stupid fool.

HAWA *(Groaning, bending over as she clutches her belly)*: You see, you see! The medicine you don't want in your sore, you shouldn't put in another person's sore. If you don't want me to say that about your mother you shouldn't have said it about my mother in the first place.

SAMSON: I can say and do whatever I want.

HAWA: You have no right to hit me either. This is not the first time you are hitting me like that. Do you think I am your football?

SAMSON: I have the right to hit you. You belong to me. You are my wife.

HAWA (*She stops crying. Stands up straight and wipes her eyes with a tip of her lappa*): I don't belong to you. I am not your wife. To whom did you put kola for me?

SAMSON: What is the difference between a *tap-to-me* and a wife? I don't need to put any kola for you. As long as you are living with me and everyone knows it, you are my wife.

HAWA: Stop calling me your wife! I am not your wife. *Tap-to-me nor to marade*! Even if I were your wife, that would not make me your property. There are other ways to treat people who don't agree with you.

SAMSON: Violence is the only way to deal with people like you.

HAWA: You are right. I have myself to blame. You wouldn't treat me this way if I had not moved in with you in the first place. My mother warned me about you; everyone warned me about you, but I did not listen to them.

SAMSON: Your mother has never liked me because I am poor. You are just like her; you are all money Fernandos.

HAWA: You have no shame. I don't love you for money. You know I forsook other men, including that moneyman in Tongo who promised me everything. I chose you even though you had nothing: no money, no certificate beyond the Common Entrance, no work, nothing.

SAMSON: If you are not a money worshipper, what are you doing with that minister?

HAWA: What minister?

SAMSON: Don't ask me what minister. Were you not in his car? What were you doing in his car if you were not sleeping with him?

HAWA: Oh, I see. So that's what this is about! I am not sleeping with him. I had never met him until today when he offered me a lift.

SAMSON: You had your two feet and your umbrella; you did not need a lift in anyone's car. I am sure he did not force you into his car.

HAWA: He didn't force me. He offered me a lift, and I took it. Nothing is going on between us. I am fed up with the way you treat me.

SAMSON: Why don't you leave if you are fed up with me? Now that you have a minister, you can go to him. He can give you what you want.

HAWA: He is nothing to me. The only one I can go to if I have to go to someone is my mother.

SAMSON: What are you waiting for then? Pack up your things and leave. If you are not going to pack them up, I will do it for you.

He proceeds to removing Hawa's clothes from the wall hanger and out of a portmanteau he pulls out from under the bed, flinging things onto the floor: three pairs or so of wax cotton costumes, one denim skirt, one pair of dungaree pants, three t-shirts, and about four or five drawers. Hawa picks everything up and stuffs them in a Ghana-Must-Go bag. She pulls out from under the bed a pair of purple Lady D's and a pair of plastic slippers. She then goes to the table to collect her lotions, eye browns, etc.

SAMSON (*He sprints to the table and seizes Hawa's hand as she picks up the Ashobi Pomade*): No, you can't take that. What do you expect me to use on my hair? Ehn?

HAWA: That is not my problem. None of these things belongs to you. I bought them with my own money.

SAMSON: I don't care if you bought them with your blood or your flesh; you are not taking the hair pomade.

They start scuffling over the bottle of pomade.

HAWA: Lef am! If yu wan mek yenki yu go get for buy yu yone.

SAMSON: I am not going to buy anything.

HAWA (*Letting go of the hair ointment*): You can have
it. You can even have the lipstick and the eye-brown
if you think they will make you a better man. If you
had shame, you would find better things to fight over.

*Hawa picks up the bag containing her belongings and
walks out of the room. Night falls suddenly.*

WORLD BROADCASTING CORPORATION: "A recent investigative report by WBC and local Salone journalists has concluded that widespread food and petrol shortages as well as the inability of the government to pay schoolteachers and junior civil servants are results of rampant corruption in the country since independence. The diamond industry, now mostly run by Lebanese and Israeli businessmen, continues to be the main driver of corruption in Salone, the report says."

ACT III: "In a Place Just Around the Corner"

<u>Spectacle 1</u>

Monrovia. A clubhouse on a beach popular with Western tourists. Inside, feet shuffling to "Pink Cadillac." Samson can be seen alone under a hut a few yards away from the clubhouse. He is throwing stones at a kingfisher hovering over the water in the distance. A man comes out of the clubhouse, dancing and singing: "I love you for your pink Cadillac/crushed velvet seats...." He joins Samson under the hut.

BOIMA: Hey Salone borbor, any luck?

SAMSON *(After a few seconds)*: No! What about you?

BOIMA: Well, I have set a trap. All I have to do now is wait.

SAMSON: James told me yesterday that one of your traps caught something. Is that true?

BOIMA: Yes and no. No, because I lost it to someone else immediately afterwards.

SAMSON: How did that happen?

BOIMA: You know the story. I think she found bigger and better than mine. Some of these women come here just for that. Can you imagine! They pay hundreds of the almighty dollar just for that! As if that is not enough, once here, they even pay you to do it. In fact, some are old enough to be your mother.

SAMSON: I know your problem, Boima. I have always told you to avoid the pretty ones; they are either already taken or being watched by others. Everywhere in the world, pretty women are like hot *akara*. They don't stay alone for long. They are out, they are grabbed. What *we* should do is focus on the others: the fat ones and the ugly ones. We must be practical, my friend.

BOIMA: Do you think a woman's physical appearance makes a difference? Some women may be ugly or fat, but that doesn't mean they are cheap. Take for example, my uncle's wife. She is not one you can even call handsome. But I tell you, my uncle ran after that woman like she was a piece of kimberlite diamond. Everyone wondered what he saw in Gedwo. One of my aunts even claimed that Gedwo had taken her brother to a *jujuman*. Personally, I don't think so. My uncle is a wise and strong-headed man that no juju can confuse. On the other hand, I know beautiful women who are...

SAMSON (*Gets up and starts walking toward the ocean, throwing stones more aggressively at the kingfisher, which eventually flies away. Boima follows him*): Listen to me. I am talking to you from experience. Look at Kanyon for example, where is he today?

BOIMA: In America.

SAMSON: How did he get there?

BOIMA: If it was through that girl, man! It is true I badly want to go to America. But I don't think I can ever open my mouth and tell someone like her "I love you," especially if I don't mean it.

SAMSON: You are still missing the point. The important thing is to achieve your goal; it doesn't matter how. As a wise man once said, "the end justifies the means!" Haven't you heard that saying before? Anyway... "I love you" is just a way to get what you want from women. You don't have to mean it. Even women don't really expect you to mean it. They just like to hear it. If I see a woman today that holds my passport to the land of Uncle Sam, no matter how ugly she is, I won't hesitate for one second to tell her: "Oh! How I love you, baby. You are as beautiful as the early morning rose. You attract me like the nectar attracts a honey bee. I want to marry you so badly I can't wait till tomorrow. So what do you say, sweetie pie, what do you say?" Once we are married and over there in America, and my papers are all in place, I will have no qualms leaving her.

BOIMA: How? I hear it is more difficult for a man to get a divorce in America than it is to survive in our countries today.

SAMSON: Yes, it is. But to every problem, there is a solution.

BOIMA: But how?

SAMSON: Why don't we talk about something else, Boima? Something more pressing.

BOIMA: Like what?

SAMSON: We have been hunting for nearly a year now to no avail. It is high time we changed terrain and tactics. Man is not born to hunt the same thing and in one place forever.

BOIMA: What do you have in mind?

SAMSON: Nothing at the moment. But I am sure something will come up.

WORLD BROADCASTING CORPORATION:
"According to reports from Monrovia, the band of armed men known as the Liberian National Patriotic Front that entered the country from Côte d'Ivoire several months ago continues to gain territory. The group's leader, an alleged American prison escapee, Charlie Singer, has said that his main goal is to free Liberia within a matter of months from what he calls the unpopular and corrupt regime of President Eskay Dho. Meanwhile, we have received unconfirmed reports of an armed incursion into neighboring Salone."

ACT IV: "A Man Came Questing"

Spectacle 1

Abidjan. High noon. Samson is alone, standing not too far from the entrance of a nightclub, wiping beads of sweat from his forehead with a handkerchief, talking to himself.

SAMSON: If what Kouamé and Lassine told me yesterday is true, I must be a really good *zouglou* dancer. Come to think of it, I don't need their opinion to know that I am a good dancer. I can feel it myself. I can see it when I look at myself in the mirror. Was I not a star of break dancing in Monrovia? How many competitions did I win there? Now it's zouglou I have to master. Even though I prefer break dancing, I have to focus on zouglou now. Break dancing is not very popular here. If I want to be known all over this city, I have to master zouglou. C'est ça le zouglou dance! I have to do it better than the Ivoirians themselves. Everyone will know me at the Caiman Club and even beyond, just as Okonkwo was well known throughout the nine villages and beyond. Wherever I go people will say: "Look! That is Samson, the Salonean who can dance zouglou better than any Ivoirian."

Samson starts jigging to a beat in his head as he wipes his forehead some more. A Ford pick-up pulls up and stops abruptly in front of Samson, with its front right tire almost crushing his foot.

POT: Na in dis!

Samson makes to run, but then he stops, reassured by the language he just heard. He recollects himself in time to answer the question from a man of medium height and weight, probably in his late fifties, with a dense whitish beard and mustache, carrying a lion-headed staff.

SAY BANA: Na yu name Samson?

SAMSON: Yes, mi na Samson!

SAY BANA: Kushe! I am Say Bana. As you can see, I am from Salone like you. Do you know Pot? *(Pointing to a man just about to jump out of the back of the truck)* He is the one who told me about you.

SAMSON: What! Paul? This guy is almost like a brother to me. Come here!

The two men hug, shake hands, and hug again.

SAMSON: Where have you been all these years, man? And how did you get the name Pot?

POT: The full name is Paul Pot. It is a long story. You will know everything later. For now, I will let the "pa" speak. Listen to him carefully, ok? He has something very important to say.

SAMSON: No problem.

Pot returns to the truck.

SAY BANA: Pot has told me a lot about you. You are the kind of people I am looking for to take part in my project. I need people with mind.

SAMSON: What is the project?

SAY BANA: I am planning a revolution in Salone. You know that country has been in a mess for a long time now. Corruption, illiteracy, immorality, corruptibility, bad governing, stealing, lack of good governance, no morality, you name it. Everyone has suffered in that country, except the big fat politicians and civil servants. Look at you! Pot has told me how much you have suffered, how much you have been humiliated. What are you doing in someone else's country when your country is rich enough to take care of you? Think of all the diamonds, the bauxite, the rutile, the fish, the gold, the gems, the barracudas, the bongas, the minnas, the iron ore... If you turn out to be what Pot told me you are, I don't see why you shouldn't be one of my right hand men. It's all up to you. I can assure you that we will succeed. We have plenty of high-level support. Charlie Singer is behind us, Braise Kompari is for us, the president of this country is helping, and above all, the great Colonel Jamahiriya is giving logistical and moral support. Will you join me?

SAMSON: I have heard you. What you have said demands serious reflection. Come back to this same spot tomorrow at about the same time. If I am here when you come, then my answer is yes.

SAY BANA: Without fail! I am looking forward to your positive answer. In the meantime, you can buy *attiéké* and vimto with this. (*He gives him a 5000-franc note*) Look at you! You are dry like *gbagbakuru bonga*! You don't have to suffer like this. Remember that.

SAMSON (*Smiles as he takes the money with both hands*): Oh! Thank you very much, sir.

SAY BANA: That's nothing. There is more of that ahead. Your future is in your own hands.

Say Bana returns to the truck. Samson goes over and says something to Pot before the vehicle speeds away.

Spectacle 2
In a room somewhere in Abidjan. Nighttime. Samson is tossing and turning on a blanket-covered straw mat on the floor, mumbling to himself. Shadows on the walls dancing in tandem with the flame from the cambo *lamp. Enter stage right, 1ˢᵗ Heart, and stage left, 2ⁿᵈ Heart.*

1ˢᵗ HEART: Think, Samson, think of what you will be in the future. Join Say Bana.

2nd HEART: Think, Samson, think of what you will do to the future. Don't join Say Bana.

1st HEART: Imagine. At this time, nobody knows you. Not even in your father's house. You can count on the fingers of your left hand the people who see you as anything. The government does not know you exist. No one respects you. Look at Hawa, beautiful Hawa. Did she not leave you for that minister? In this world, if you don't have money and power you are nothing. Today, Mr. Honorable Minister is enjoying your Hawa. Your sweet sweet Hawa. People like the minister must pay for what they have done to people like you.

2nd HEART: True, people like the minister must pay for their misdeeds. But does it have to be through the means you are contemplating? Think of all the people like you who will suffer because of your actions.

1st HEART: Don't worry about other people. Their problem is not your problem. *Dis nah monki duniya!* You should worry only about your own troubles.

2nd HEART: It makes no sense to set your entire house on fire just because you want to get rid of two or three impertinent mosquitoes. If you do, peace of mind will never be yours again.

1st HEART: Peace of mind and happiness, like *keinda* and *ogiri*, are mere condiments. With power and money, you don't even need to go to the market yourself to purchase them; your servants can easily take care of that.

2nd HEART: Think of all the children and your fellow citizens, Samson.

1st HEART: Think about the power you will have. Open your eyes, your mind's eyes, and look at the future. You will be famous, known beyond your wildest imaginings.

2nd HEART: You will be known at the four corners of the globe, true, but the log, no matter how long it has been in the river, will never become a fish.

1st HEART: I can see the future spread out before you in the horizon like a newly crafted bamboo mat. No, more beautiful than that; like a huge Turkish rug like the ones you see in the Abidjan shops.

2nd HEART: It seems my words in your ears, Samson, are like talcum powder on the back of a tortoise. One last piece of advice before I leave you: Don't be like the man who lies on his back to piss at the sky because he is mad at it. Good night and God be with you. (*Exits*)

1st HEART: Empty proverbs that don't mean anything! Imagine, no history books on Salone, on West Africa, indeed on Africa as a whole, let's even say the world, will be complete without your name in them. No plays, no novels, no poems about the country will be composed without you as its hero. You will forever occupy a prime position in the company of great men. I can see you are exhausted. I will take my leave now. Have a good night!

1st Heart exits as Samson begins to snore noisily.

WORLD BROADCASTING CORPORATION: "At the start of the second year of the Salone civil war, a cohort of young army officers calling themselves the Salone National Provisional Governing Council, and led by a 27-year-old army captain known as Melville Streeter, has overthrown the government of President Sahid Binkolo. Massive popular show of support for the putschists has been reported throughout the country, including at Mount Aureol College, the main campus of the University of Salone."

ACT V: "Unleash the Dogs of War!"

<u>Spectacle 1</u>

Somewhere in Salone. When the spectacle opens, Samson is alone in a room. Outside, in the distance, 'Revolution Time' by Culture could be heard. Physically, Samson has not changed much since we last saw him. Remarkable about him now are his accoutrements and his immediate surroundings. He is dressed in Desert Storm-style military fatigues complete with a black beret, a holstered pistol, and glossy black boots. Samson is sitting on a swiveling black leather chair behind a large mahogany desk such as you would find in the offices of top diamond dealers in Kwedu Town. He is spotting a pair of dark Ray-Ban glasses. Sprawled out in front of him is a large map of Salone. The entire Eastern region, as well as parts of the south, are colored in red. The remaining areas, including the western promontory, appear precariously close to the red zone. To the right of the map sits a satellite telephone. Samson pulls a small jewelry box out of his right breast pocket, opens it and empties its contents on the map--about four or five glittering stones, each roughly the size of a quarter Béghin-Say sugar cube. A sudden gust of wind blows in through an open window, animating the map. Samson scowls, flips open a Swiss pocket knife, and stabs the map in place. For a few seconds, he plays with the stones, which have now assumed a crimson tint. He smiles, puts them back in the box, and returns the box to his pocket.

SAMSON (*Gets up and starts pacing and talking to himself*): I have everything: money, power, respect.

Everybody fears me now. And one day the entire country will be mine. But until I have Hawa and the minister together under my control, until I can show them I am somebody, I will not be satisfied, I will not rest.

SAMSON (*Heads toward the door, but changes his mind, then returns to sit behind his desk*): Angel!

ANGEL (*off stage*): Yes, brer!

A timid young man, dressed in faded jean pants and a t-shirt comes running in with an AK-47 swinging from his shoulder like a pendulum out of control.

SAMSON: Didn't I tell you to only address me as Captain?

ANGEL: Yes capay, I mean yes Captain, sir!

SAMSON: The next time you fail to address me as Captain, you will be demoted to *fontoba*; do you understand?

ANGEL: Yes, Captain, sir.

SAMSON: Any news?

ANGEL: There is no news yet, Captain, sir.

SAMSON: What do you mean 'no news yet'?

ANGEL: We have tried hard, but we have not been able to locate her yet.

SAMSON: What about that stupid minister? Any word on him?

ANGEL: Yes, Captain. Our sources tell us he is in Freetong, like most of his colleagues.

SAMSON: Then Hawa must be with him.

ANGEL: I am not sure sir. So far, no one has reported seeing them together.

SAMSON: Are you saying I am a liar? I know they have been, and are together as I speak. Didn't I tell you this was a priority? Stand down!

ANGEL: Yes, Sir, Captain. (*Salutes and exits.*)

SAMSON (*To himself*): The rest of this damn country must fall soon. I must get to Freetong. Soon. Whatever it takes.

Spectacle 2
Same. Samson is still talking to himself. Enter 1st Heart and 2nd Heart.

1st HEART: So how are things going, my dear friend?

SAMSON (*Jolted*): Oh. It's you. Not bad at all. Things are going very well. Just look at this map.

1st HEART (*Does not look at the map*): But I told you everything would be fantastic.

2nd HEART: It is not too late, Samson.

SAMSON: Oh, you again! Not too late for what?

2nd HEART: To stop what you are doing.

1st HEART: Don't listen to him, Samson. He is a distraction.

2nd HEART: You can still choose a different path.

SAMSON: Which path?

2nd HEART: The path away from blood and destruction.

SAMSON: I am trying to rebuild this country. Sometimes, you have to destroy what doesn't work in order to build something good.

1st HEART: You are listening to him, Samson!

SAMSON: Not really.

2nd HEART: You ought to listen to me, Samson.

SAMSON: I am not listening to you.

2nd HEART: Well, I will bother you no more then.

SAMSON: Good idea.

2nd HEART exits.

Spectacle 3

Same.

1st HEART: Good riddance! There are more important things to attend to. You know the World Broadcasting Corporation journalist is going to be here any time now.

SAMSON: Yes, yes. I had forgotten about that.

1st HEART: That means you have to take a new name. A 'nom de guerre' by which you will be known. Every great fighter has one. Nkrumah was called "Osagyefo," Mandela was "Madiba," that guy in Iraq was called "Chemical Ali," Idi Amin Dada was "Conqueror of the British Empire," so on and so forth. You should choose a short but powerful name. You know this is your first real interview.

SAMSON (*Pensive*): A name, a name. That's a brilliant idea. What about the Great Mountain Lion?

1st HEART: Yes, the king of beasts, lord of the jungle, etc. The lion is too popular. There is the Lion of Judah, the Lion of this and that. Even football teams use the name lion, like Indomitable Lions, the Lions of Teranga, etc… The lion's renown is not a result of any real heroic or historical exploits due to the animal. It is a figment of people's imagination. Be imaginative. Think of another name. A name that is less obvious, yet more realistic and powerful.

SAMSON: What about uhm, uhm… American Eagle. You know the eagle. It is a powerful bird that swoops down and collects its prey like a big child does his feeding bottle. *(He demonstrates)*

1st HEART *(Laughing dryly)*: Beautiful, but inappropriate. I don't like the choice for two reasons. First, animals like that don't exist in Salone. That is a symbol of America. Second, the eagle, like the lion, is already too well known. Everybody wants to be an eagle or a lion. Think harder.

SAMSON *(Thinking hard)*: Do you like Rambo or the Mighty Elephant?

1st HEART: Everyone wants to be Rambo. As for the elephant, it is too obvious. It is too big. It can't go anywhere it wants to. Look at you. Think of how easily you move around in the forest and bushes, through large and little spaces alike.

SAMSON: Well, I can't think of anything else.

1st HEART: What is Salone's nickname?

SAMSON: Lion Mountain. In fact, that's why I chose The Great Mountain Lion in the first place. I wanted to be patriotic.

1st HEART: Correct. But Salone has another nickname, one that makes people shiver upon hearing it.

SAMSON (*Visibly frustrated*): I give up.

1st HEART: I will give you a clue. Salone got that nickname because of a creature, a tiny tiny insect every Salonean knows and dreads. Everyone in the world knows about it. Books have been written about it. Billions and billions of dollars have been spent to eliminate it. All in vain.

SAMSON: Really?

1st HEART: Yes! That tells you how powerful this creature is despite its puny size. It always leaves its victim weak and helpless. In Salone, and in many other countries, it is the biggest cause of death, especially among children.

SAMSON: Yes! That's the kind of creature I want to be. It is just like me, skinny, disrespected, but powerful. Stupid of me not to have thought of it right away *(hitting his forehead with the palm of his right hand)*. What creature is it?

1st HEART: Think harder.

SAMSON *(Pensive)*: The mosquito! *(He jumps out of his chair, causing it to swivel)*. The mosquito! The mosquito!

1st HEART: That's it. So where do Rambo, the lion, the elephant, and the American eagle stand now?

SAMSON: Nowhere near the mosquito. *(Becoming rather serious and ceremonious)* From this day forth, I will be addressed as Mosquito. Field Marshal Mosquito.

1st HEART: Field Marshal Anophelius. Anophelius sounds better, don't you think?

SAMSON: Yes, absolutely. Just like Julius Caesar. *(Ceremoniously)* Field Marshal Anophelius!

1st Heart disappears just as a knock is heard on the door.

SAMSON: Yes! Who is it?

ANGEL: He is here, Captain. The journalist is here.

SAMSON: Right on time. Bring him in!

Spectacle 4

Same.

JOURNALIST: Good afternoon, Captain.

SAMSON: Consider yourself lucky, for you are the first to know this. You are going to let the whole wide world know that from now on I will be known and addressed as Field Marshal Anophelius.

JOURNALIST: Yes, Field Marshal Anophelius. But if I may ask, sir, how did you come to choose that name? The world might like to know.

SAMSON: Of course. You know how much I love my country. A love that will make me destroy anything and anyone that stands between me and her. I chose the name for obvious patriotic reasons. As you are aware, the mosquito is the most notorious creature in Salone. I have been hated and pursued. From the days of the White man to the present, different forces and many countries have used their resources just to eliminate me. But I always come out victorious. I saved Salone from colonialism. I will always be victorious. I am the Omega and the Alpha, the beginning of the end. My name and power will never die.

JOURNALIST: Super! You could not have chosen a more appropriate name.

SAMSON: That's exactly what I thought. Now, shall we begin the interview?

WORLD BROADCASTING CORPORATION: "The leader of the United Salone Revolutionary Party (USRP) has been arrested and detained in Nigeria. Field Marshal Anophelius, recently interviewed by our own West African correspondent, is expected to become the new battlefield commander of the rebel organization."

ACT VI: "No Haven for the Wayfarer"

Spectacle 1

Just before sunset. Hawa, her mother, and her brother arrive at Honorable Minister's house. They are visibly exhausted, dust-covered. The boy, about 11 or 12 years old, is bare foot. The house is wrapped in a high concrete wall topped with barbed wire. An armed guard stands in front of the large metal gate.

GUARD: Stop! Where are you going? What do you want?

HAWA: We are here to see Honorable Minister.

GUARD: Is the pa expecting you?

HAWA: No!

GUARD: Then he cannot see you.

HAWA: Please, I am begging you. We have to see him.

GUARD: What do you mean?

HAWA: This is my mother and this is my little brother. For the past few months, we have been running from rebels. On foot. By God's help, we have made it to Freetong, the only safe place in the country today. We know no one else to go to in this town. Honorable Minister is our only hope.

GUARD (*Looks them over, his eyes softening a bit*): What is your name?

HAWA: My name is Hawa.

GUARD: Does Honorable Minister know you?

HAWA: He may remember me from when we met a few years ago. But let him know we are from his constituency in Kono.

GUARD (*Glances at his watch*): Ok. Just wait here.

Guard enters through the gate and closes it behind him. Hawa and her mother sit on the ground. Her brother remains standing, sucking his left thumb while rubbing his large navel with his right hand, his eyes darting from left to right. Guard returns.

GUARD: I have told the pa you are here. He didn't say anything. But you can continue waiting. If you are lucky, he will agree to see you after his dinner.

HAWA: Tenki tenki, mi broda. May God bless you.

<u>Spectacle 2</u>
Hawa and her family are still where we last saw them at the end of the previous spectacle.

HONORABLE MINISTER (*Calls the guard*): Guard, who wants to see me?

GUARD: It is a woman, her mother, and her brother, sir. They say they are from your constituency.

Hawa and her mother get up.

HONORABLE MINISTER: Tell them to come to the veranda and wait for me there.

Guard: Yessa.

The visitors walk up to the veranda. Honorable Minister comes out.

HAWA: Good evening, sir.

HONORABLE MINISTER: Who are you?

HAWA: I am Hawa. This is my mother, and this is my little brother. We are from your constituency in Kono.

HONORABLE MINISTER: I have already been told. But do I know you?

HAWA: Maybe you remember me. We met once, a few years ago.

HONORABLE MINISTER: I have met many women. I don't remember the majority of them.

HAWA: You once gave me a lift to my house on Nyandebo Street in Kwedu. It was raining that day.

HONORABLE MINISTER (*Thinking*): Nyandebo Street... Hawa... On a rainy day... Ah! I remember now. You are that funny girl. The one who refused my offer of help back then.

Hawa doesn't say anything.

HONORABLE MINISTER (*He looks at her from head to toe; then licks his lips*): You haven't changed much despite your haggard look. Not at all. You are the same pretty girl I saw that day years ago. What can I do for you?

HAWA: We need help, sir. We have nothing. We have nowhere else to go.

HONORABLE MINISTER: Is that so?

HAWA: Please, sir. Help us.

HONORABLE MINISTER: What a small world! You could have been my girlfriend or my wife, you know. It is too late for that now. However, being the good person I am, I will give you the chance to salvage a bit of the offer I made you back then. You know what to do if you need my help.

He turns around and walks into the house, not inviting the visitors to follow him.

WORLD BROADCASTING CORPORATION: "Sixteen hours GMT. This is the WBC. Here are today's top headlines: Rebels of the United Salone Revolutionary Party have reached Waterville, just miles from Freetong. Expert war watchers believe it is just a matter of weeks, or even days, before the forces led by Field Marshal Anophelius enter Salone's embattled capital. Meanwhile, foreign embassies have issued what they call their last evacuation warning to their citizens in the country. Elsewhere in the world, the OTNA has vowed to put an end to the ethnic cleansing taking place in the former Yugoslavia. According to the organization's Secretary-General, 'Western powers cannot sit idly by and allow such savagery characteristic of other places to unfold in the very backyard of the Civilized World.'"

ACT VII: "Thus Sayeth the Lord: 'Let my People Go!'"

Spectacle 1

Samson is alone, in the same place we last saw him. Reclining on his chair. Angel comes running in.

ANGEL: Field Marshal! Field Marshal, sir!

SAMSON: What's the matter?

ANGEL: Good news, Field Marshal.

SAMSON: What is it?

ANGEL: Hawa has been spotted.

SAMSON (*He jumps out of his chair*): Where?

ANGEL: In Freetong.

SAMSON: Is she with the minister?

ANGEL: Yes, Field Marshal.

SAMSON (*To himself*): I knew it! I knew all along that she was with that minister.

ANGEL: What do you want me to do, sir?

SAMSON (*Doesn't hear Angel. Pacing*): I knew she was lying when she said there was nothing between her and the minister. Now is my turn. Both of them will soon feel the weight of my power.

ANGEL: Field Marshal, sir!

SAMSON (*Startled*): What?

ANGEL: Is there anything you would like me to do?

SAMSON: Yes! The time has come for us to take Freetong. You know that, right?

ANGEL (*Giddily*): Yes, Field Marshal.

SAMSON: When we enter Freetong, there is one and only one thing I want you to do.

ANGEL: Anything you want, Field Marshal.

SAMSON: Whatever you do, make sure the minister and Hawa don't get away. You understand?

ANGEL: I understand, Field Marshal, sir.

SAMSON: That's all for now. Stand down. And let the troops know I will address them soon. Remember also to alert our boys in Freetong about our plans.

Angel exits the scene as Samson returns to his chair, visibly excited.

Spectacle 2
Singing and dancing are heard off stage. A ragtag group of fighters enters the stage, wielding an assortment of guns, RPGs, machetes, and sticks in the air excitedly, dancing and singing.

Tidae na dae den go sabi we
Den waya
Den waya
Den waya den go sabi we tidae

Tidae na dae den go sabi we
Den waya
Den waya
Den waya den go sabi we tidae

Samson struts out of his office and joins them in the dance. After a minute or so of dancing, he leaves the group and climbs on a makeshift dais cobbled together from tree trunks. He waves his hand and the group stops the singing and dancing and stands at attention.

SAMSON: Today indeed is the day they will know us.

FIGHTERS: Indeed, Field Marshal.

SAMSON: Who is there to stop us?

FIGHTERS: No one.

SAMSON: I didn't hear you. I am asking: Who is there to stop us?

FIGHTERS (*Louder*): Nobody!

SAMSON: What shall we do to them when we catch them?

FIGHTERS: Chop them!

SAMSON: What?

FIGHTERS: Kill them!

SAMSON: Again!

FIGHTERS: Finish them!

Samson descends from the dais. His fighters lift him up in the air and resume their singing and dancing.

Sidon dae
Sidon dae
Fil mashal sidon dae
Na yu want

Sidon dae
Sidon dae
Fil mashal sidon dae

Na yu we want

<u>Spectacle 3</u>

The scene opens sometime before sunset. A range of almost bald hills, interspersed with houses of various sizes and shapes overlooking the serene ocean below. On top of one of the hills can be seen a long line of people, flanked on both sides by several boys and a few girls, in their early to mid-teens. With the exception of one, all the teenagers are wearing bandanas around their forehead; some of the bandanas are imprinted with stars and stripes, the others are simply plain red, or black, or stained. Some of the boys and one girl are carrying RPGs or AK-47s. One boy is carrying a JVC camcorder. An older boy, likely in his late teens and obviously their leader, was wielding a rusty axe in his right hand and a can of Heineken in his left hand. On his forehead and upper arm are strips of insulation tape, his eyes dark red. He sways on his legs like someone trying to balance himself on coil spring. Between him and the line of people is a tree trunk covered with bits of flesh, bone, and congealed blood.

CAPTAIN KUT'AN: For those who don't know me, let me introduce myself. My name is Albalau. I am the captain of the Mountainside Boys and Girls Squad. The supreme representative of Field Marshal Anophelius here. Yes, I am the leader of the most powerful squad of young fighters in the world. And my name is Albalau. You all know what that means? If you don't know, no problem. I will give you the benefit and the doubt. I am a rich man. I have many names. If it is easy for you, call me Captain Kut'an, alias Rape. Ha ha ha ha. Yes, the cutter of hands and the raper of wives and daughters. The cutter of hands, yea, *(dancing)* and the raper of women and girls. All the women, all the girls, they are my wives. You *(pointing at a woman probably in her early thirties)*, step out of the line and go over there. You are in luck, and you know why? I have chosen you to be my wife for tonight. What was I saying? Oh, yes! The best in the world. These hills here are my territory, my kingdom. I, I mean I *(beating his chest with the can of Heineken, spilling beer on himself)*. I am the boss here, the king of this republic. Ha ha ha ha ha. *(He drinks from the can and then throws it at the line of people)*. Look at me *(wielding the axe rather precariously)*. Can you do what I am doing? Yeah, I feel good. I feel good tadadadadadada... I am the boss. I am going to deal with you all and send you with a message to your president in Guinea... your future is in your hands. Ha ha ha ha... Let's see how you are going to carry it. Killgore!

KILLGORE: Yes captainkuttanrape.

A boom box toting ragamuffin jumps forward.

CAPTAIN KUT'AN: Let the music play on, let the music play on play on everybody sing everybody dance...we going to partae... come on now... come on and sing with me... I can't hear you... louder.... Stop! Put the Tupac cassette. Ain't mad at cha! Now everyone dance to my man, Tu-paaaaac. Tu-pac in the hooooooouse. Yea, that's what I'm saying! (*After a minute or so*). Ok, stop! Now, everyone, sing and dance with me: "we want peace… we want peace… rebel na we padi… govment na we enimi… rebel na we padi, govment na we enimi… we want peace ay, we want peace oh…" Stop! Stop! Stop! You are terrible singers and dancers. I am not happy about that. You are going to pay for that. First in line!

A girl, wearing a teddy-bear backpack and carrying a grenade-tipped RPG on her right shoulder goes to the man at the head of the line and orders him to put his right hand on the tree trunk.

MAN (*Weeping*): Please, I beg you. Don't cut my hand. I have a wife; I have two children and my parents to take care of. In fact, they are all here. I am begging for all of us.

DOGBOWUSU (*She presses her RPG to his temple*): Obey me and keep quiet, you stupid fool. Put your hands there or I will blast you.

CAPTAIN KUT'AN: No, don't waste my grenade on him… In fact, leave him. I will deal with him and his family later. I will give him special treatment. (*He moves up and down a stretch of the line, pointing randomly at people with his axe*). You, no you, no you, no…

He stops when he comes up to a girl of about ten. Looks at her, squints several times, shakes his head wildly. He grabs hold of her hand and starts dragging her toward the trunk.

GIRL: Please, broda, don't hurt me. Do, I beg you.

CAPTAIN KUT'AN: Don't call me brother, I don't know you.

GIRL: Yes, you know me. I am your little sister. Don't you remember me? We are from the same mother and father. Just look at my face again.

CAPTAIN KUT'AN (*Looks at her, squinting and shaking his head vigorously*): No I don't know you. Dogbowusu, do you know this girl who says I am her brother?

DOGBOWUSU (*Without looking at the girl*): No, captain, I don't know her.

CAPTAIN KUT'AN: So she must be lying. For that, she is going to pay double. I hate liars.

GIRL: No, I am not lying. My name is Mameh, your name is Osman, our mother's name is Yema, and our father is...

CAPTAIN KUT'AN (*He slaps her*): Shut your stupid mouth! I don't know any of those people you are talking about. And for your information, my name is

Captain Kut'an! One more word and you are dead. Dogbowusu, if she utters one more word shoot her. *(Pointing to the trunk)* Put your right hand there. In fact, put both hands. Put the left on top of the right. Yes. The right over the left and over the right....

GIRL *(Closes her tear-filled eyes and complies)*: Okay.

CAPTAIN KUT'AN *(Looks at the axe, then flings it away)*: On second thought, Killgore, gimme the power saw.

KILLGORE *(He starts the saw and gives it to Captain Kut'an)*: Here it is, capay!

CAPTAIN KUT'AN *(Revving the saw)*: Cameraman, are you ready? Everybody look and enjoy. I order you to open your eyes and watch. This is going to be a good film. Field Marshal Anophelius will like it. After three. *(Raises the running saw)*. Count with me: one, two...

Light fades. Screams reverberate up the hills and down, finally dissolving with the last rays of the setting sun into the crimson-orange glow of the ocean below.

WORLD BROADCASTING CORPORATION:
"Lawlessness and food shortages continue to be the order of the day in Salone since the military coup in May of this year. As most sectors of society, including state functionaries, teachers, students, and civil society groups continue their boycott of the Armed Forces Governing Council government, soldiers, rebels, and sobels routinely harass the general population. To make matters worse, no foreign government has yet recognized the junta. This could be the first time in modern history that a regime has not been recognized by any other."

ACT VIII: "And the Twain Shall Meet Again"

Spectacle 1

A lavishly adorned mansion. Outside, armed men patrolling. Samson could be seen in a bedroom lying on his back, with his left hand supporting his head on a plush pillow. He is wearing a pair of boxers and a t-shirt. The almost silent purring of an invisible air-conditioning system can be heard. A minute or two pass. Suddenly, the scene changes. The room and everything in it, except Samson, have become multiple times their size. Samson gets up with a start, sitting upright in the bed. His eyes closed. Terrified! Tiny rivulets of sweat run down his face and arms. He screams: "Please, please, stop it!" *When he finally opens his eyes, he is in the middle of a desolate landscape. He turns around to run back into the house, but there is no house. All around him scorched earth, remnants of houses, trees, and human bodies. In the distance, amidst the haze, a figure appears, humming happily to himself.*

1st HEART:
To ti yo to
To ti yo to
Yu mama bin dae tel you sae
Yu papa bin dae tel you sae
Tranga yayse nor gud
You nor yeri
Tranga yayse nor gud

...

SAMSON (*A glimmer in his eyes*): Oh, thank God! You could not have come at a better time. Please help me!

1st HEART: Pardon me, do I know you?

SAMSON: Yes, you are my friend. Don't you remember me?

1st HEART: No, I don't recall ever meeting you. Who are you?

SAMSON: I am Samson, your good friend.

1st HEART: Samson! Samson! Doesn't ring a bell.

SAMSON: I am Anophelius. Don't you remember me? Field Marshal Anophelius! You gave me that title.

1st HEART (*His chin in his hand, thinking. Talks to himself*): Hmm… Anophelius! Anophelius! That is the name of an insect, a very dangerous insect. How could a human being take such a name? (*Turns to Samson*). In any case, I don't have time right now to remember. I have an important matter to attend to. Good-bye.

1st Heart resumes his cheerful humming as he saunters away. Samson runs after him and reaches for him, but the latter has already vanished into the surrounding haze.

Spectacle 2

Honorable Minister's house. Samson is pacing up and down a dimly lit living room, waving a pistol agitatedly. Honorable Minister is on the floor, naked but for a pair of underwear. Hawa is sitting in a loveseat. She is pregnant. Angel stands guard at the door.

SAMSON: Who got you pregnant?

Hawa looks at Samson, and then at the minister, but says nothing.

SAMSON: I am talking to you, Hawa. Who got you pregnant?

The minister tries to speak, but Samson strikes him on the mouth with his pistol.

SAMSON: Shut your mouth. I wasn't talking to you. (*To Angel*) Take him outside and tie his hands behind his back. I will deal with him later. On second thought, let him stay here.

SAMSON (*Walks over to the minister, aims the pistol at him, and turns to Hawa*): Now, answer my question or I will shoot him. Who got you pregnant?

HAWA: Don't shoot him. He is the father of the child I am carrying.

SAMSON (*Visibly furious*): I knew it. I was right when I said you were sleeping with him.

HAWA: No, you were not.

SAMSON (*Grabs Hawa and lifts her up from the seat*): So how did he impregnate you if you were not sleeping with him?

HAWA: It is true I carry his child. It is also true I wasn't sleeping with him when you and I were together, or even after that.

SAMSON (*Drops Hawa back on the seat*): You have his child and you still tell me you were not sleeping with him?

HAWA: The war came and we lost everything. We had nowhere else to go. I did what I had to do.

SAMSON (*Irate, poking Hawa's belly with his gun. Hawa seizes his hand in an effort to stop him*): That child in your belly is supposed to be my child, not his.

HAWA: Stop, you are hurting the child. You are hurting me.

SAMSON: I won't stop. And I don't care about the child. He is not mine. As for you, you still belong to me. Pregnant for a minister or not, you are coming with me.

He drags her towards the living room exit.

HAWA: Coming with you where?

SAMSON: Wherever I feel like taking you.

HAWA: I am not going with you anywhere.

SAMSON: Why not? Because of the stupid minister? Ok. (*Let's go of Hawa and goes to the minister*) So this is why you don't want to come with me? (*Shoots the minister in the foot*) I will shoot him in the other foot if you still refuse to come with me.

Goes back and grabs Hawa.

HAWA (*Struggling to free herself from Samson's grip*): You can do whatever you want; it will be on your head, not mine. I don't belong to you and I am not going with you anywhere. Let go of me!

SAMSON: Stop fighting.

As he tries to switch hands, the pistol goes off, and the bullet hits Hawa in the belly.

HAWA (*Moaning*): No! No! What have you done? My baby. My baby. No! No!

Hawa's voice fades as she collapses to the ground.

SAMSON (*He picks up Hawa's limp and bloodied body, screaming*): Nooooooo...! I have killed Hawa. My beautiful Hawa. No, I just killed my one and only Hawa.

He lays her gently on the loveseat.

SAMSON: Where is that goddamn minister? This is entirely your fault.

He goes over to the minister and fires several rounds into him.

WORLD BROADCASTING CORPORATION:
"According to our reporter in Freetong, ECOMOG forces led by Nigerian troops have now succeeded in pushing rebel forces and their allies outside of Freetong city limits, thus paving the way for the return of the elected government from exile. The people of the coastal city and the country at large are hopeful that this development will force the USRP to return to peace talks with the government and other stakeholders."

THE END

Author Bio

M'Bha Kamara (pen name for Mohamed Kamara) is Professor of French and Africana Studies at Washington and Lee University, Virginia, USA. He has a BA and a Diploma in Secondary Education from Fourah Bay College (the University of Sierra Leone), an MA from Purdue University and a PhD from Tulane University (both in the United States). Mohamed's teaching and research interests include French language as well as French and Francophone literatures and cultures, with specific focus on African and Eighteenth-century French women writers, French colonial education, and human rights. In addition to short stories, he has published articles on human rights, the African child soldier, French colonial education, and other areas of African literature. Mohamed is currently completing a monograph on the representation of the French colonial school and the invention of the African bourgeoisie in Francophone sub-Saharan literature.

CPSIA information can be obtained
at www.ICGtesting.com
Printed in the USA
BVHW032012231121
622367BV00004B/247

9 781300 584162